EXTREME LIFE CYCLES

PARASITOID WASP

WRITTEN BY
E.C. ANDREWS

KidHaven
PUBLISHING

Published in 2025 by
KidHaven Publishing, an Imprint of
Greenhaven Publishing, LLC
2544 Clinton St., Buffalo, NY 14224

Written by: E.C. Andrews
Edited by: Noah Leatherland
Designed by: Amelia Harris

Cataloging-in-Publication Data

Names: Andrews, E.C.
Title: Parasitoid wasp / E.C. Andrews.
Description: Buffalo, New York : KidHaven Publishing, 2025. | Series: Extreme life cycles | Includes glossary and index.
Identifiers: ISBN 9781534547049 (pbk.) | ISBN 9781534547056 (library bound) | ISBN 9781534547063 (ebook)
Subjects: LCSH: Wasps--Juvenile literature. | Parasitoids--Juvenile literature.
Classification: LCC SB945.W3 A537 2025 | DDC 595.79--dc23

Manufactured in the United States of America

CPSIA compliance information: Batch #CSKH25
For further information contact Greenhaven Publishing LLC at 1-844-317-7404.

Please visit our website, www.greenhavenpublishing.com.
For a free color catalog of all our high-quality books, call toll free 1-844-317-7404 or fax 1-844-317-7405.

Find us on

IMAGE CREDITS

All images are courtesy of Shutterstock.com, unless otherwise specified. With thanks to Getty Images, Thinkstock Photo and iStockphoto. Cover – Ernie Cooper. Recurring Images – meechai39, mentalmind, Alfmaler, ReVelStockArt, Macrovector, Eightshot_Studio, Miloje. 2 – Ava Peattie. 4–5 – PCH.Vector. 6–7 – Ernie Cooper, Lenti Hill. 8–9 – Richard Stephen, Erik Karits. 10–11 – Carlos Pereira M, Dan Shachar. 12–13 – Ava Peattie, Thongthaeng. 14–15 – Stephen Bonk, SIMON SHIM. 16–17 – Victor Suarez Naranjo, Eduardo Dzophoto. 18–19 – Tomasz Klejdysz, DeRebus. 20–21 – Vinicius R. Souza, InsectWorld. 22–23 – Cosmin Manci, InsectWorld.

CONTENTS

Words that look like this can be found in the glossary on page 24.

WHAT IS A LIFE CYCLE?

All living things change and grow throughout their lives. Their lives are split into different stages. This is called a life cycle.

Most living things start off small. They grow up, get old, and one day, they die. During their lives, animals often continue their life cycle by having <u>offspring</u>.

WHAT IS A PARASITOID WASP?

A parasitoid wasp is a type of flying insect. Parasitoid wasps live all over the world. They are usually found in fields and gardens where there are lots of flowers.

THERE ARE THOUSANDS OF DIFFERENT PARASITOID WASP SPECIES.

Parasitoid wasps are very small. However, they can be very dangerous to other insects. Some types of parasitoid wasps can reproduce very quickly. The way they do it is quite scary!

REPRODUCTION

Mating is when a male and female animal of the same species come together to make offspring. Most animals have to mate in order to have offspring. However, female parasitoid wasps can reproduce without a male.

WHEN PARASITOID WASPS MATE, THE MALE **FERTILIZES** THE EGGS.

Whether a parasitoid wasp is male or female depends on whether its parents mated or not. Female wasps hatch from fertilized eggs. Male wasps hatch from unfertilized eggs.

LAYING THE EGGS

The female wasp lays her eggs in a very strange way. First, the female wasp finds a living insect. This insect is called the host.

THE HOST CAN BE AT ANY STAGE OF ITS LIFE.

The mother climbs onto the host and injects her eggs into its body. The eggs live inside the host's body. The host stays alive. The host's body protects the eggs until they are ready to hatch.

HATCHING

Once the eggs are laid, the mother leaves. Baby wasps hatch from the eggs while still inside the host. Baby wasps are called larvae. The larvae live inside the host's body for several weeks.

The larvae need food to grow. They are fed by the host in which they hatch. They start to eat the host from the inside out. The host is alive the whole time!

LARVAE EMERGE

The larvae keep feeding on the living host. When the larvae have grown big enough, they emerge from the host's body. They use their very sharp teeth to burst out.

The host is paralyzed as this happens. Sometimes the host dies. Sometimes the host lives. Whether they die or not, the larvae sometimes eat what is left of the host.

COCOONS

Once the larvae have emerged from the host's body, they spin themselves a cocoon. A cocoon is a silky case that protects them as they grow.

PARASITOID WASP LARVAE SPIN THEIR COCOONS NEXT TO THE HOST.

Inside the cocoons, the larvae grow into adult wasps. It can take a parasitoid wasp around six days before it is ready to come out of its cocoon.

THE ZOMBIE GUARD

If the host does not die and is not eaten by the larvae, it sometimes guards the larvae. The host is hurt and a bit paralyzed, but it still protects the wasp larvae like a zombie!

Sometimes the host sits on top of the larvae to protect them from predators as they spin their cocoons. It watches over the cocoons until it dies of starvation.

ADULTHOOD

Parasitoid wasps are fully grown adults when they come out of their cocoons. They are able to fly as soon as they emerge. They fly away and leave the dead host behind.

ADULT PARASITOID WASPS LIVE ON THEIR OWN.

Adult parasitoid wasps are less scary. Most of them feed on pollen and nectar, which are found in flowers. Until they're ready to reproduce again, that is!

THE CYCLE CARRIES ON

When parasitoid wasps are ready to reproduce, they will find a host like the one in which they hatched. They will inject their eggs into it and have offspring of their own.

Parasitoid wasps do not sting. They cannot harm humans. They help plants by controlling bugs that harm them. Their life cycle may sound scary, but it is an important part of nature.

GLOSSARY

EMERGE to come out from inside of something

FERTILIZE to make an egg grow and develop

HATCH to come out of an egg

INJECT to push something else into the body using a sharp, thin object

INSECT an animal with six legs and three body parts

OFFSPRING the young of an animal or plant

PARALYZED unable to move

PREDATOR an animal that hunts other animals for food

REPRODUCE to have offspring

SPECIES a group of very similar animals or plants that can create young together

STARVATION dying from not eating enough food

INDEX